Rookie Read-About® Geography

Living in the Arctic

By Allan Fowler

Consultant
Linda Cornwell, Coordinator of School Quality
and Professional Improvement
Indiana State Teachers Association

Children's Press®
A Division of Grolier Publishing
New York   London   Hong Kong   Sydney
Danbury, Connecticut

Visit Children's Press® on the Internet at:
http://publishing.grolier.com

Designer: Herman Adler Design Group

Library of Congress Cataloging-in-Publication Data

Fowler, Allan.
    Living in the Arctic / by Allan Fowler.
      p.   cm.   —   (Rookie read-about geography)
    Summary: Discusses people who live in the Arctic regions of the
world and how it affects their lives.
    ISBN 0-516-21561-2 (lib. bdg.)   0-516-27084-2 (pbk.)
    1. Arctic peoples Juvenile literature. 2. Arctic Regions Juvenile
literature. [1. Arctic peoples. 2. Arctic Regions] I. Title.
II. Series.
GN673.F68   2000
998—dc21   99-38877
                                                              CIP

On a cold, snowy day, people sometimes say, "It's arctic weather." Do you know where the Arctic is?

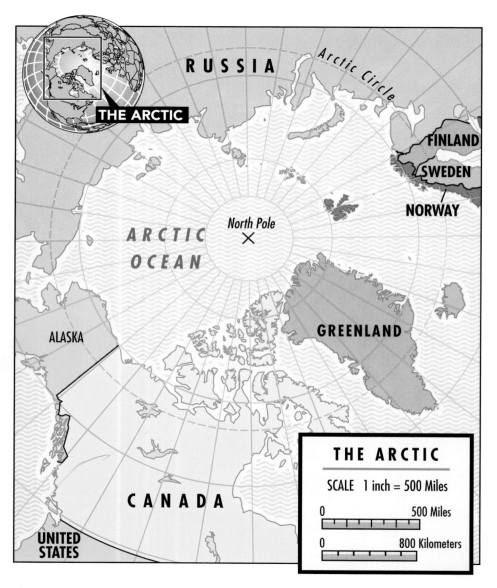

THE ARCTIC

RUSSIA

Arctic Circle

FINLAND

SWEDEN

NORWAY

North Pole
✕

ARCTIC
OCEAN

GREENLAND

ALASKA

CANADA

UNITED
STATES

THE ARCTIC

SCALE 1 inch = 500 Miles

0   500 Miles

0   800 Kilometers

4

The Arctic Circle is an area of land and water around the North Pole.

Parts of the United States, Canada, and other countries are in the Arctic Circle. But most of the Arctic is a body of water called the Arctic Ocean.

Almost all the Arctic
Ocean is covered with
a thick ice cap.

The edges of this ice
cap melt in summer.

Ships can then sail
along the coasts of
the Arctic lands.

In summer, you can see the sun nearly all night long. This is because the North Pole is facing the sun during the summer.

There is little sunlight during the Arctic winter. This is because the North Pole is facing away from the sun. Days are almost as dark as nights.

Much of the land within the Arctic Circle is called tundra. Snow covers the tundra in winter. The soil is frozen.

Only the top twelve inches of soil thaw in summer. Then grass, mosses, and shrubs can grow—but not trees.

Frozen tundra in winter

Tundra in summer

People find ways to live
in cold Arctic regions.

Do you ever wear a parka—
a jacket with a hood?

The first people to make
parkas were probably the
Inuit (EE-neu-eet). Inuit
live in the Arctic regions
of Canada and Alaska.

Inuit girl wearing a parka

Inuit man in a kayak

Inuit travel on water in boats called kayaks (KIE-aks), or longer boats called umiaks (OO-me-aks). They build igloos of hard snow.

Igloo

But more often, Inuit homes are made of stone or covered with animal skins. Inuit also live in towns.

Inuit home

Soapstone carving

Inuit artists make beautiful carvings out of whalebone, walrus tusks, or a rock called soapstone.

The Sami are people who live in the Arctic parts of Russia, Finland, Sweden, and Norway.

Some Sami tend reindeer. They get milk and meat from the reindeer. They use the hides for clothing.

Sami woman with a reindeer

Some other Arctic animals are polar bears, musk oxen, Arctic foxes, and hares.

All have heavy coats to keep them warm.

Musk oxen

Arctic fox

Walruses

Seals, walruses, and whales
swim in the Arctic Ocean.

Many birds nest in the Arctic, such as puffins, loons, and ducks.

Puffins

People must be clever and animals must be tough to live in the Arctic cold.

Words You Know

Arctic

igloo

Inuit

kayak

30

musk ox

puffins

Sami

tundra

walruses

31

Index

About the Author

Allan Fowler is a freelance writer with a background in advertising.
Born in New York, he now lives in Chicago and enjoys traveling.

Photo Credits

©: Corbis-Bettmann: 11 (Galen Rowell); Dembinsky Photo Assoc.: 25 top,
31 top left (Dominique Braud); Peter Arnold Inc.: 13, 20, 31 center right
(S. J. Krasemann), cover (Michael Sewell); Photo Researchers: 17, 30 top right
(B & C Alexander), 8 (Tom Hollyman), 3 (Brenda Tharp); Robert Fried
Photography: 23, 31 center left; The Stock Market: 27, 31 top right (Charles
Krebs), 7 (Torleif Svensson); Tony Stone Images: 29, 30 top left (Ragnar
Sigurdsson), 25 bottom (Art Wolfe); Wolfgang Käehler: 15, 16, 19, 26, 30
bottom right, 30 bottom left, 31 bottom.

Map by Bob Italiano.